salmonpoetry

*Publishing Irish & International
Poetry Since 1981*

ABOUT MARY MELVIN GEOGHEGAN'S EARLIER COLLECTIONS

'Mary Melvin Geoghegan's style is quirky as she dislocates syntax and punctuation, tapping into private levels of our awareness.'

NOEL MONAHAN

'There is a highly-distilled, imagist quality to the work which can be very effective.'

NESSA O'MAHONY

'The words are bleached to the bone by the clear light of her observation and experience. Grief and joy are balanced with one another to give us at the end a collection that is rich with redemption and hope, where each moment has been made sacred.'

GERALDINE MILLS

'Mary Melvin Geoghegan has an original use of language. She is gifted with imagery; her engaging economical playfulness delivers up riches, getting to the heart of every subject'.

NUALA NÍ CHONCHÚIR

'Mary Melvin Geoghegan's poetry is tender and compelling; she examines the finest minutiae of family relationships and the inevitable passing of time, tranforming the personal into something universal. I'd compare her voice to William Carlos Williams – the poems having a hidden strength that underlies their illusory sense of effortlessness.'

EAMONN LYNSKEY

As Moon and Mother Collide

MARY MELVIN GEOGHEGAN

Published in 2018 by
Salmon Poetry
Cliffs of Moher, County Clare, Ireland
Website: www.salmonpoetry.com
Email: info@salmonpoetry.com

Copyright © Mary Melvin Geoghegan, 2018

ISBN 978-1-912561-19-3

All rights reserved. No part of this publication may be reproduced or transmitted in any form or by any means, electronic or mechanical, including photography, recording, or any information storage or retrieval system, without permission in writing from the publisher. The book is sold subject to the condition that it shall not, by way of trade or otherwise, be lent, resold or otherwise circulated without the publisher's prior consent in any form of binding or cover other than that in which it is published and without a similar condition, including this condition, being imposed on the subsequent purchaser.

COVER IMAGE: *Bernard Canavan*
AUTHOR PHOTOGRAPH: *Shelly Corcoran*
COVER DESIGN & TYPESETTING: *Siobhán Hutson*

Printed in Ireland by Sprint Print

Salmon Poetry gratefully acknowledges the support of
The Arts Council / An Chomhairle Ealaíon

i.m. Mary Ellen Melvin

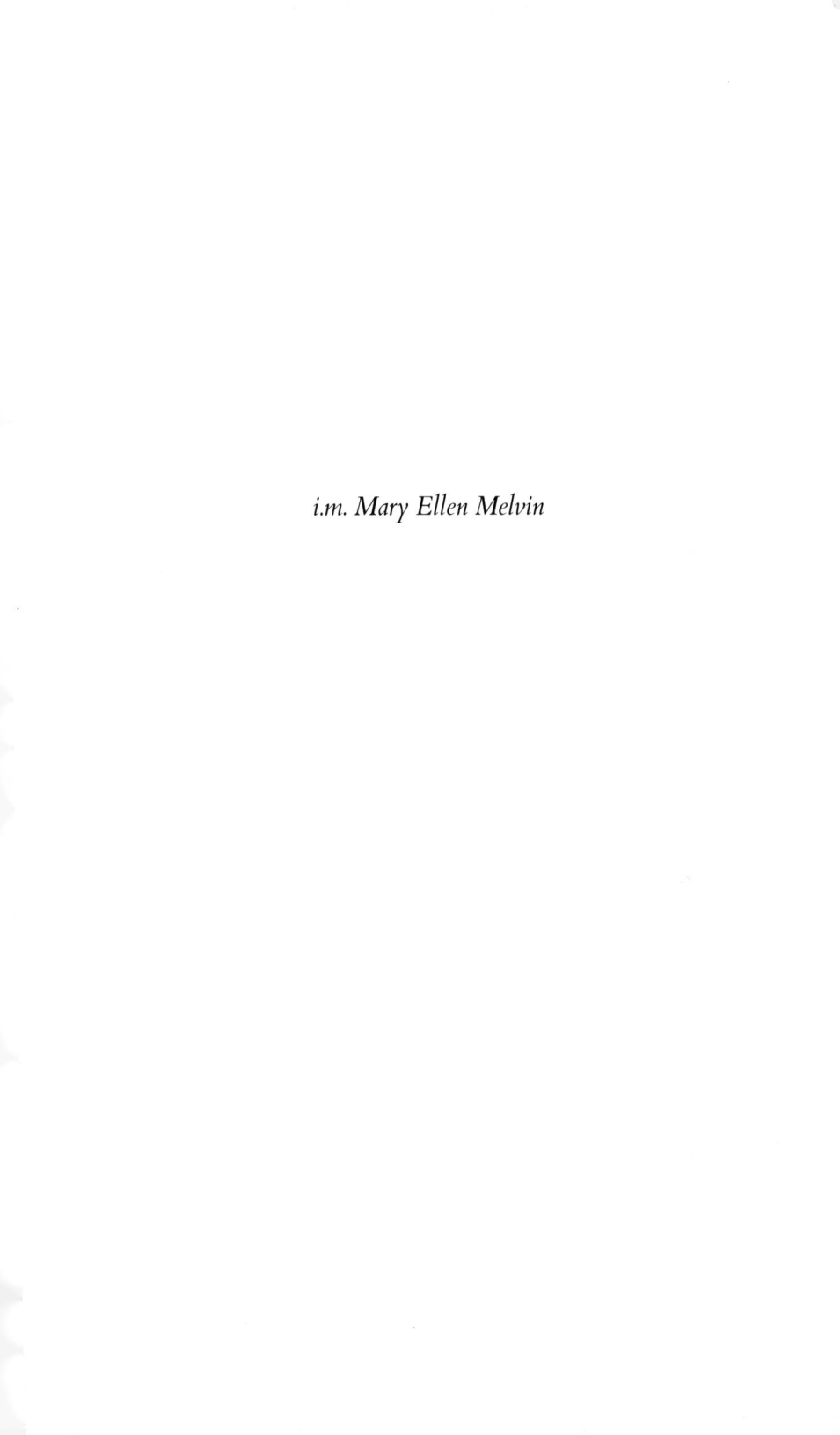

Acknowledgements

Some of the poems in this collection have been published in *Poetry Ireland Review* No. 117, *Cyphers, Skylight 47, Crannóg, The Stony Thursday Book* (2015), *Riposte, Rubies in the Darkness* (London), *A Labour of Love* (Ontario, Canada), *Alternating Current* (Louisville, U.S.A., 2018), *The Longford Leader, Live Encounters, Siarscéal Anthology, Centenary in Reflection* (2016), and *Respond* (to Michael Croghan's photograph, Longford Arts Office, 2014). "Rededication of St. Mel's Cathedral" was re-imagined as a short film, entitled *Time Travel* by Seamus Clarke, as part of the Poem to Film Project organised and funded by Longford Arts Office (2015).

Contents

As Moon and Mother Collide	11
Hoping	12
A Response to Hearing Mid-Term Break Again	13
In Arnotts	14
Home for Christmas	15
A Lifelong Reich	16
Out of the Ordinary	17
Looking to Camera	18
A Sorry Like That	19
Good News, Bad News	20
Strand Road	21
Installing the New Printer	22
The Geography of a Writer	23
Something Out There	24
The Mall	25
I'll Never Forget	26
Climbing Vesuvius	27
From the Centre of the Earth	28
In a Gift of Stickers	29
Glastonbury 2013	30
Out of the Skies Over Kazakhstan	31
'My Roscommon'	32
'Ploughed Field'	33
Holding On	34
Visiting Knock	35
A Group of Cavalry in the Snow (1800)	36

Could it Be	37
After Readings at Crannóg	38
West Side Story	39
The Man Who Collapsed Into Monet	40
For All Seasons	41
On a Visit Back to Dublin 11	42
Rufus Wainwright Drops In	43
The Fiddle in Longford	44
The New Bird Table	45
A Hero	46
In the Reina Sofia in Madrid	47
'Picture with Three Spots'	48
Looking for my Grandmother	49
The Boy at the Hospital Window	50
In a Footnote	51
Ghost of the Mart	52
Another Summer	53
My Beads	54
The Wedding	55
The Leather Boots	56
Over Lough Arrow	57
The Pile of Bricks	58
It's Perfect Don't Move!	59

Will Leave it all in Yesterday	60
Rembrandt Needed the Money	61
The Slippers	62
Ealasaid	63
Down in the Crypt	64
Caravaggio Finds Mary Again	65
The Rain at the Window	66
Angela's Hydrangeas	67
Sacrifice of Interest	68
On a Visit to Cabra Castle	69
The Pidgeons Helicopter	70
Take a Look	71
Trying to Find My Whereabouts	72
The Lost Fields	73
Ten Years to Pluto	74
Cordoba Today	75
In a Curve of Hope	76
On the Rededication of St. Mel's Cathedral	77
A Rib from a Stone Vault	78
The Clock	79
Airstrike	80
At The Thiepval Monument	81
Searching for Áine	82
About the author	85

As Moon and Mother Collide

I take out my wedding dress
and the shoes my mother bought,
shake out the collapsed veil
and wind it round my throat.

I release the tension in the veil
and allow it fall all over the secret,
hoping my throat will open again.
Still, guilty of something.

Hoping

In Nassau Street to-day
I almost saw my sister Imelda.

A Response to Hearing Mid-Term Break Again

i.m. Mary Ellen Melvin

I see my mother crying
outside Holles Street,
waiting in the snow.
The green Ford van had broken down.
I sit beside my father
in the borrowed replacement
at the Baby Hospital across the road
looking down on Breda,
born with water on the knee
making one leg shorter than the other.
She was the eldest of the little ones
who spent years in and out of hospital
having surgery on both knees.
Now, each can hold its own.

In Arnotts

the feeling of my mother.
I let myself graze along the First Communion rack.
Thinking of the cost, and how much
saving up, the same then as now.
Heavily pregnant and
five already at home –
she gave the best.

Home for Christmas

i. m. Tommy Cox

In Multyfarnham cemetery

standing beside Robbie

I'd forgotten

in the excitement of my son's returning,

how for him –

it was always, and perhaps always will be

the news of Tommy's drowning

on Christmas Eve.

A Lifelong Reich

from Fiona Sampson

of unexpected gifts.
Opening the greenhouse door
the frost putrefies the last of the tomatoes.
Except for
a trail of opened flowers
behind the rotten cucumbers,
innocent of Winter.

Out of the Ordinary

I heard –
actor Stephen Rea on the radio
tell how his mother was difficult.
She barely spoke to him
and in later years
before he'd visit
would drop in on a neighbour.
Once, she reassured him
promising to pray for both.
As usual his mother never spoke
suddenly, he began to feel a heat
coming through from the wall next door.
Then his mother said out loud
'take a seat son, your hands are cold.'

I read –
about the painter Eugene Delacroix
how, the water drops on the bodies
of the damned souls in 'The Barque of Dante'
are formed in separate touches
of green, yellow and red that blend
not on the canvas
but, in the eye of the viewer.

Looking to Camera

George Mitchell, the former US Senator returns
to Northern Ireland, with his fourteen year old son
born the year of the Good Friday Agreement:

I catch their trip on tv
watching the discrepancy slip between
a father old enough to be a grandfather and a son
caught in an explosion of understanding.
The day ends in Omagh, George says –

'I only know two people here.
One, a schoolgirl blinded in the bombing
I remember each day when
I call my daughter Claire'.

A Sorry Like That

She told the reporter:
she'd never heard, a sorry like that.
Listening in the Gallery of the Dáil
with the survivors of the Magdalene Laundries
while, the head of a Government
goes down on both knees.

Good News, Bad News

from Leicester —
Richard III has been unearthed
the monarch's bones were found
beneath a car park.

from Leicester —
glancing through the death notices
I see an old friend has died suddenly.
'Pamela, I'm sorry it's been so long.'

Strand Road

for Marian and Pauric Melvin

Now, all your own.
I never thought
invited out to sea
from a favourite armchair
in your new home –
how, that window could frame
for all of us
the possibility of a future
as sure as the tide.
Beyond the fields of Roscommon
and the clear skies of North County Dublin.

Installing the New Printer

I was devastated
when the flashing icon warned
the cylinder was leaking ink.

The man in the shop didn't say much
except make sure to play the cd before
attempting the manual connection.

Between conversations on the phone
dashing back and forth checking the screen –
I went to bed leaving it up to God!

First thing next morning back at the screen
all went smoothly down to the last
pop up saying – connected.

Trying out the new printer
back on the phone, instead of one printer
I had five on the system.

Another day spent deleting the extra ones –
couldn't work out where the paper went,
back on the phone again.

The first printed pages arrive
all over the floor, miraculous as snow.
I'm in a flurry of relief.

The Geography of a Writer

Started in Longford
after I first left Dublin and
was embraced by a kind, vast sky,
elegant cow-parsley saluted
a new Spring, and full green fields
were borrowed straight from the page
of a Thomas Hardy novel.

And when page and pen began
I found myself in a tradition
supported by writing groups: Cúirt
in Galway, Strokestown in Roscommon,
Oliver Goldsmith in Ballymahon and
Maria Edgeworth in Edgeworthstown;
in the library requested books and
news of readings on the noticeboard.

From Longford tentatively began
to send out work and discovered
the alchemy of a county seemed
to strengthen, enable words to find
their own weight elsewhere.
Now, another generation is flexing
its writing muscle far and wide
while, all the living and the dead
read on.

Something Out There

from the window
of the back bedroom in Abbeycartron
across the football pitch,
an early Spring evening –
its afterbirth and light
just delivered.

The Mall

I know this place
from when I first pushed a buggy
heading to feed the ducks.
With only the trees and river
and that full sweep of sky
still answering the need
under the wing
of any passing bird.

I'll Never Forget

the first sight
of the Amalfi Coastline
written by an ancient sea
and the doll's house view from the boat.
A landscape thrown up
from eruptions under the moon,
conquered and cultivated
in the perfection of lemon
and olive on the tongue.

Climbing Vesuvius

clutching the rope
till, the sky opened up
and the clouds were a crown.
While the mountain
that had evacuated itself
so long ago stood
almost, on the sidelines
as the sky and clouds
grabbed the limelight.

From the Centre of the Earth

two lumps of rock

sit on the mantelpiece

giving no hint

of enormous rage.

In a Gift of Stickers

for Joan McBreen

Chagall arrived today –
in a booklet of stickers.
Almost in the same way years ago
my father pulled out the artist
just as I was about to leave.
Flicking through –
I become his subject.
He invites me to choose a city
colour, century and time of day.
On reflection, I tell him;

'paint me in North County Dublin
in amongst the cowslips
sitting beside my brother
up in Kettle's field on a Sunday;
our father and sisters down at the water
and our mother resting
on a cloud.'

Glastonbury 2013

Mick Jagger looks, except for the face

as skinny as ever, the other band members

fortunately not, though probably normal for blokes their age.

'You Can't Always Get What You Want'

hoping their next song will be –

and as soon as that cord thumps out

I'm back at the Office Christmas party

dancing with the Jesus Christ look alike

a string of blue beads like sweat at his throat

and some leather contraption on his wrist.

And as the familiar loop explodes again and again,

I jump up twisting and shaking

turn up the sound to my full

SATISFACTION!

Out of the Skies Over Kazakhstan

i. m. Jo Cox MP

Astronaut Tim Peake parachutes
from the Soyuz capsule along
with two colleagues, as a young woman
walks behind and stitched to her shirt
a white, blue and red tricolour
the flag of the Russian Federation.
With a broad smile –
she comes to assist
their first moments back on earth.

The day before the landing
in the town of Birstall, England
all gathered to honour –
a force of nature, a five-foot-bundle
of Yorkshire grit and determination.
Who never knew out of the skies
of a home town, her last moments
were coming.

'My Roscommon'

begins outside Ballaghaderreen

approaching the sign for Lisacul

before the bridge, my mother falls from a bike

breaks a front tooth;

past the church where they were married

turning right always a little unsure –

to the fork in the road

over another bridge;

and then every bush and blade of grass

becomes all who have gone before

and will come in the future;

under a Silverfield sky

the colour and mood intensifies

as I approach Pat's place

I'm grateful –

on the way back

I stop at the graveyard

just inside the gate, greet Uncle Joe

and further along peep in at Grandparents

safely tucked up

in eternity.

'Ploughed Field'

Tidying up, I come across
a field in Poulaphuca in Co. Wicklow,
wrapped up and stacked away
with dried earth, like pepper
crushed against the glass.

Today, Seamus Heaney died,
the only consolation is finding
the 'Ploughed Field' painted by John Woodfull,
and I'm back in Poulaphuca
beside my father fishing.

Holding On

as a tooth breaks on an apple.
I can't escape the grief leaving
Streedagh Strand in Sligo and
all those lost from one of the Armada ships,
having managed to swim to shore
were slaughtered just as they drag
their bodies from the water.

I could have swallowed the tooth.
My tongue can't leave the crater alone –
smooth as the stones beneath my feet
marking a Spanish mass grave.

Visiting Knock

for the first time since –
in the church Harry Clarke's Mary
is a touchstone.
Through my open fingers
the back of an elderly woman
is bent over a walking frame,
scraping her way to a front seat.

In the gathering of leaving
we're beside one another.
And all she is, and has received
is there on a face as young as it's old –
radiant as the Virgin Mary's
coming through the stained glass.

A Group of Cavalry in the Snow (1800)

Ernest Meissonier

lies open on the hall table,
highlighting Dessoles, perched on a cusp of cliff.
His cocked telescope like an eagle regurgitating
the terrain back to General Monreau.

That painting first enthralled a long time ago:
its freezing stillness and pallor of premonition,
the precision of hussar uniforms and horses,
lifted me from a grey Winter's day in Dublin
to an Napoleonic campsite, and all
those poor devils waiting in the snow.

And that posture of anticipation
in the captured snow and sky
still, shivers before —
the bloody victory of nightfall.

Could it Be

all this talk of earth

as pure potential,

and we're the Higgs Boson

giving mass to happiness

just as that particle behaves

itself in quantum physics?

After Readings at Crannóg

Crane Bar — 25th October 2013

Next morning
full Autumn, in Eyre Square
the rain lashes down.
Looking out the window
the tree closest to me
is having a hard time
holding on to its leaves –
which, as we speak are being
collected by Leonardo da Vinci
while he's thinking about the roots.
Roots, which will have to support
growth, spreading across centuries
quietly absorbing the sunlight
in the silence of Sforesco Castle.
Now, the world holds its breath
beneath layers of whitewash
as those leaves reappear.

West Side Story

Tonight in Dublin
a New York skyline opens.
I can hear my father's first cries
and grandparents gulping in the new arrival
as a gang of dancers step out.

Earlier in the day
rummaging through old bank statements
I come across
a half-torn photo of a baby
kept in his wallet.

Now, singing along with Maria
next minute in tears
watching —
love, dead in our arms.

The Man Who Collapsed Into Monet

in the National Gallery, in Dublin

says, he suffered from angina and

went on to have a quadruple bypass after his dip

in Monet's 'Arenteuil Basin with a Single Sailboat.'

Both have since recovered.

The frame has been repaired,

the sea is calmed, and sailboat reupholstered,

the sky has been touched up here and there

perhaps, a shade more serene than previously intended.

Forgiveness is reflected in the presence of the

recuperating bush that's learning how to breathe again

grateful, that posterity won't be denied.

For All Seasons

Stopping at the traffic lights
I'm trying to hide
from that black plastic bow
on the electrical shop door.
Almost, at the same angle
as the sagging shopfront.
The owner is on everyone's lips.
In our last conversation over the new kettle
as the debit card was being processed
there was a pause –
before it returned –
before he was taken.
After he'd wished us all
Good Day!

On a Visit Back to Dublin 11

Beyond the Botanic Gardens
the 83 bus crawls up
Constitution Hill to the lights.
The struggle for the 19 was lost.
Along Tolka Estate taking a short cut
by a new enclosure of neat homes and gardens.
The O'Connell Monument in the distance
grows like a half fat Spire against the Dublin Mountains.
The wall at the bottom looks uncertain
till it opens on to Tolka Cottages and
our old family home across the road –
new front door and windows.
Ash Wednesday, and the couple in front
were once next door neighbours –
he upright as the Garda Sergeant
and she as homely as remembered.
Áine beside me is deep in prayer
as the sister of a friend awaits surgery.
The priest, who gives out the ashes
once herded cattle for my father, on Jamestown
looks the same as ever.

Rufus Wainwright Drops In

on Dublin after a quick cavort
at the Venice Carnevale and as his
fingers and voice touch the piano and mic
it's almost, in the same transit of pleasure
as the lyrics of Leonard Cohen.
But, without the wisdom of age
he still exudes an other wordily sheen
that resonates in the timbre of presence
and notes that seem to roll between heaven
and self-deprecation: in a review in The New York Times
of his new opera which finished in the words
'chic and pointless'.
Now, begins life again in a song.

The Fiddle in Longford

was always in my kitchen

under the chin of musician Irene Guckian

until it raised the roof

and longed to be installed

along the new N5 bypass,

charming the eyes

of every passing motorist.

The New Bird Table

for Kevin

The consultant said

surgery was the best option.

On the way home

I remembered the bird seed.

Out there in the garden my ex

was sawing and making

the past between us.

A Hero

for Dr. Muhammad Taufigal Sattar

I saw him coming

down the hospital corridor,

the Neurosurgeon

talking on the radio

of his wife and children

killed in Leicester

burned out accidently;

telling, how he'd discovered

after six weeks that he

was enabled to resume,

and while scrubbing up

preparing for surgery,

constantly prayed

for a good outcome.

In the Reina Sofia in Madrid

it was all so amazing.
The architecture of the building
the glass, steel and reinforced concrete
colliding in a pleasing aesthetic.
And suddenly just round the corner
there's Guernica –
and I'm in the scream of a woman
searching for a missing eyeball
while a severed nipple lies crushed
on the floor, negating all previous
impressions of its monochrome.
As on the day the artist's fury
first scythed through the pain.

'Picture with Three Spots'

Wassily Kandinsky

in the Thyssen-Bornemisza, Madrid
is framed in a moment that begs to be
photographed as Katie steps into the picture.
Round the corner my son hears the flash –
frowns, then relents in an expression
as memorable as the painting.

Looking for my Grandmother

i.m. Brigit Regan

is proving more difficult
not, the actual whereabouts
but, the disruption of a
settled narrative more taut
as her memory is evoked.

In Cathy's burnt out kitchen
only the face on the fridge survived –
the photograph of the Grandmother
I'd been looking for –
her open smile and happy eyes
a legacy to us.

And still my mother's voice:
'it could be a lovely thing
on a Summer's day to return,
even as I got away'.

The Boy at the Hospital Window

is my brother standing
in plaster up to both knees.
I'm not allowed in to see him.
He waves down
his face pressed against the glass.
The blond curls
as on the day
he was taken from me.

In a Footnote

struggling through Cherubini's Requiem
in The Sylvia Dawson Hall in Longford
on those after Christmas nights when the tempo
strained with so many vowels and consonants:
discovering what the choir was attempting
was first performed in Paris in the Winter of 1817
in the crypt of St. Denis, in memory
of Louis XVI and Marie Antoinette.
The executed King and Queen, we learn
had been attended by l'Abbé Edgeworth.
Who fled to France as a child
when the family changed religion.

And this made all the difference
in a footnote –
in St. Mel's Chapel
two centuries later.

Ghost of the Mart

is running down Phibsboro in Dublin
in amongst the poems and traffic.
They could be the Shorthorns and Black Pollys
I remember from childhood.
No sign of the Friesian who also arrived in the post
running around the mart
about to be launched.

Another Summer

for Dermot Healy

Another Summer and another poet

is taken too soon.

And suddenly his gift

is felt as loss causing a desperate

search for all his books.

Opening 'The Ballyconnell Colours'

and finding his inscription

was always there for me.

Waiting for us all –

'winds that drive men crazy

are ecstasy for birds'.

My Beads

coil, as on a beach of repetition

almost as ponderously

as the endless offerings

of the sandworm.

The Wedding

for Karina and Liam

Under a canopy of Wicklow trees
I see my brother tense as his daughter
makes a vow that's already arching
far out into a future family tree.

On either side her grandparents
have just descended from the sky,
while the bridegroom's broad gleam
is confirmation the angels
are on side.

The Leather Boots

Visiting the Luan Gallery in Athlone
with its river of wall, I'm remembered
when this building was a library.
And I got the job, and a newly delighted husband
ran across the road to buy a pair of boots.
Later, I struggled with the switchboard –
and the day, Councillor Mary O'Rourke
appeared as pristine as this new space
with its iconic Louis Le Brocquy's 'Táin,'
and 'Cúchulainn' and the 'Army Massing.'
Marching to the same war cry echoing
across Gaza, Iraq, Syria, Ukraine.

Over Lough Arrow

the chieftain stands,
guarding the wildflowers and crops
and the farmer closing the gate
stooped over all he loves.
I pick one of the flowers
then you join in and soon
there's a bunch ready –
you, wonder if they'll survive the journey.
I'm looking at them now
up on the mantlepiece
as upright as when
they were broken.

The Pile of Bricks

in Florence slumped against the wall
is the work of Anthony Gormley.
And the person I'm passing now
sleeping in the doorway.

It's Perfect Don't Move!

response to Michael Croghan's Photograph

Somewhere in Dublin
on a bench –
the sun shadows down
and the leaves are still stuck in place.
Your spotted, no caught
just, after you'd put down the bag
opened your shirt collar
plonked the hat on your head.
Did you know your being set up?
in the next moment
company will arrive
but, don't worry
they're just included
in case I might need a sandwich.
My lens is focused on
your far out beyond,
feet squarely sandaled to the ground,
adjustable walking cane –
I like the detail.
And your hands resting
in all the given and received
almost as if –
Godot's round the corner.

Will Leave it all in Yesterday

how Claire washed grapes
set the table, cut bread
turned on the fire.
And I sat back
into her view of Dublin.
And slowly the hearth
expanded
till everyone
was home.

Rembrandt Needed the Money

In October 1662 –

the chilled Amsterdam nights

were draining light from the afternoons.

Rembrandt sold his wife's grave

when bubonic plague raged again in the city.

Men with rounded bladed shovels

turfed out Saskia's bones

making room for the next lodger.

It was not so very shocking,

for the fate of mortal remains

was of no concern to the Church.

But, God knew

Rembrandt needed the money.

The Slippers

are left —
as he'd stepped out of them,
inside the front door
into a life resumed miles away.
I don't seem able or
want to disturb them.
It's not long till Christmas,
closer to the time
I'll slip them upstairs.

Ealasaid

Around the corner
of the train station in Longford Town,
you arrived
in bright yellow.

As we embrace
you tell me
your new coat is attracting
all the bees.

'They think I'm a flower'.

Down in the Crypt

of St.Mel's Cathedral in Longford
Stefan Emmelman is photographed
helping a large statue back to life.
I can't see the face
but, the head is bent
whispering to him.
He has already restored all the angels
and even created two new ones,
just, waiting to soar

'as it was in the beginning
is now
and will be forever more'.

Caravaggio Finds Mary Again

the Magdalene after several centuries
he'd misplaced her behind all the gossip
scandal and just plain fascination.
Now, he slightly adjusts the ecstasy
so it could be understood
or taken for childbirth.
Making her comfortable
he mixes the pigment
to moisten her lips.
The brush trembles
as he paints open
our eyes.

The Rain at the Window

is bursting to get in.
I think I'll open the window
see, where it wanders
give it the run of the house
upstairs, between the sheets.

Angela's Hydrangeas

Last Summer –
I admired her huge white hydrangeas.
Thinking of all the gaps at home
after the two culling Winters.

Another year –
opening the front door
she's there with a youngster in each pot,
slipped and taken to heart –
marked destination
here.

Sacrifice of Interest

'Once the prey has been killed
the animal's intestines and blood
are removed and mixed with bread
to be used as bait' –

The introduction to a Goya hunting scene
in the Prado in Madrid leaves me outside:
saying goodbye, and the wrench in his handshake
shooting through on the Metro
for Parque Quintana de los Molinos,
through a mist of almond blossom.

On a Visit to Cabra Castle

in Kingscourt –

we push through the front door

finding a corner

a respite from January.

Then the staircase beckons

to an empty dining room

tables set, almost, expecting –

And out on the corridor

stopped in our curiosity

mottled behind a huge glass frame

an Irish tricolour, perhaps a century old.

Still reeling from the strain

of those bullet holes.

The Pigeons Helicopter

over Sackville Street, mindful
of a retrieved Easter Monday
straight from 1915 –
the year before all changed.

My grandfather up from Roscommon
parents still waiting to be born.
The carousel spins
the 'Road to the Rising'
swollen with a crowd
borrowed from another century.
And the whole day long
the sun shines down on children –
high on their fathers' shoulders –

peering into the distance
remembering where they were
when Ireland will celebrate
fifty years on.

Take a Look

next time when in St. Stephen's Green
at the duck-keeper's house,
standing right beside one of the lakes
just, as it did in 1916.
When Jack Kearney the duck-keeper
fed the ducks, twice a day.
As both sides agreed
to stop firing.

Trying to Find My Whereabouts

in Madrid –
inside Museo del Prado
the light of Georges de la Tour
caresses 'The Newborn Child.'
Later, upstairs El Greco
catches my attention
in the gaze of 'Saint Francis of Assisi'
and like a kite I'm blown.

Visiting my son's apartment outside Madrid
we ramble through the noticeboard –
including photos from childhood
sitting on Santa's knee in the Grotto with his brother.
Then he slips an arm around my waist
and I'm home again.

The Lost Fields

She reads, her home place

the fields with names

running down to the river.

Listening, I get lost

as I climb over the gate

looking for our fields.

Till, I remember

how our parents spread the cloak

so each is never

without shelter.

Ten Years to Pluto

along with a death, divorce and
the highs and hollows of expectation.
And then to our sheer amazement –
ahead of the calculated time
by two seconds,
the New Horizons spacecraft
caught sight of Pluto.
And from billions of kilometers
Earth was brought closer
to the vast within
and beyond.

Cordoba Today

dropped through the letterbox.

In a fridge magnet with stars

falling from the ceiling of Mezquite Cathedral

and a greeting –

that stuck straight to my heart.

In a Curve of Hope

the day heats up
sitting under the white birch
in the July of the garden.
The firetail creeps closer
and the wedding cake tree
despite the brambles
is trying to be visible.
There's work to be done –
but, sitting near you
there's a clearing.

On the Rededication of St. Mel's Cathedral Longford

17th May 2015

Waiting in the choir –
as the Cathedral begins to fill.
Thinking, how the foundation stone
was taken from the historic ruins in Ardagh
over a century and seventy five years ago.

Now, standing with forty thousand others
in a wet field, as the first sod is cut.
Today, it's under a silver tabernacle
above polished marble
on this new Ascension Day
as future generations descend;

remembering its own history
from the great famine to the Fire of 2009;
how, it was restored and music charmed
the angels back to the ceiling.

A Rib from a Stone Vault

A rib from a stone vault
rests against the east wall down
in the crept of Glasgow Cathedral.
I run a finger along the stone groove
and feel the comfort of centuries.
That certainty of endurance
grips me again in the nave
in front of the Millennium Window
created by John K Clark.

Outside towards the Necropolis
I'm escorted up the hill by the rib –
and introduced to Glasgow's founding fathers
with John Knox towering above the wind
still holding forth.

The Clock

for Peter

a gift from his mother.
Brings him up the steps
of St. Mel's Cathedral in Longford.
Taking off the cellophane
inside, running up the aisle
as on so many Sundays.
Now, finds the batteries
and adjust the hands
to his own time.

Airstrike

Omran Daqneesh
is beamed across the world.
The five year old boy from Aleppo
sitting on an orange ambulance seat
plucked from the rubble of his home.
His hands caught in his lap
feet stretched out, blood and dust
screening his face yet, it's the innocence
in his eyes that burns the retina.

At The Thiepval Monument

1st July, 2016

Near the river Somme
a hundred years to the day
the rain drops down
in amongst the white birch trees.
The illusion of time
as darkness falls
almost, complete.

Searching for Áine

up in Glasnevin Cemetery.
I must have got it wrong
was it the end of the wall
or the railings?

Anyway, you know I'm here.

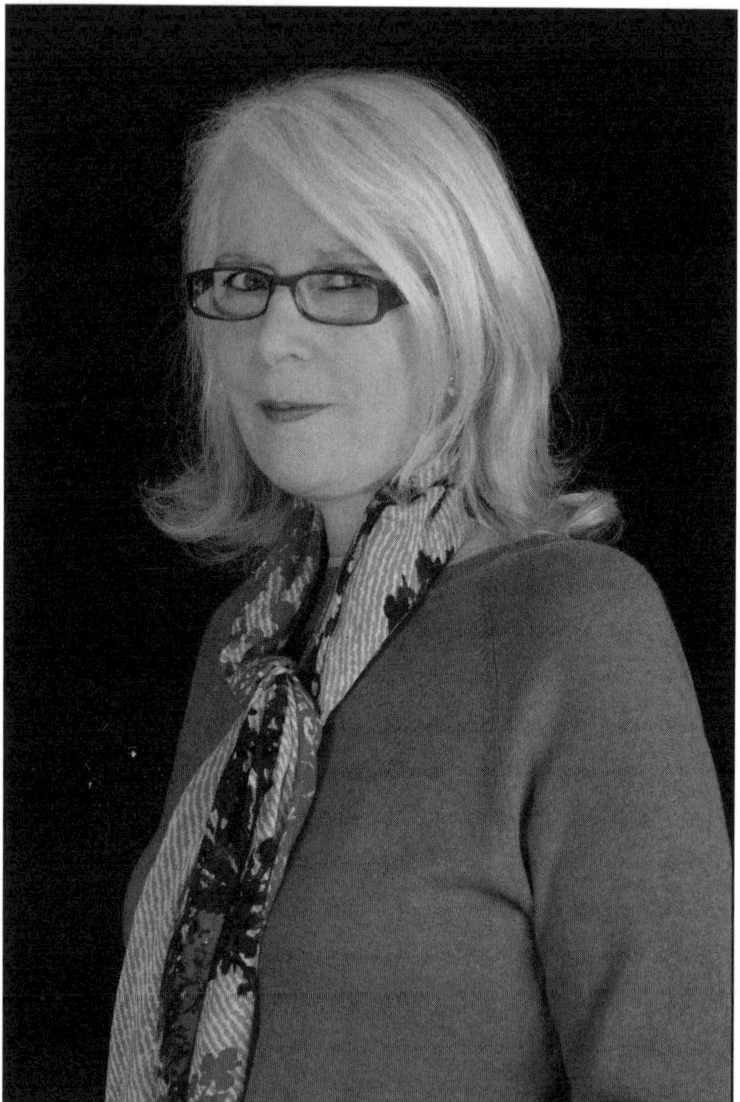

MARY MELVIN GEOGHEGAN was born in Dublin and lives in County Longford. She was an associate editor of the annual *Eurochild Anthology of Children's Poetry* (Bradshaw Books). She has four previous collections of poetry: *Say it Like a Paragraph* (2012, Bradshaw Books, Cork); *When They Come Home* (2008, Summer Palace Press); *Abbeycartron Epiphanies* (2005, Lapwing Publications); and, *The Bright Unknown* (2003, Lapwing Publications). She has edited three collections of children's poetry: *Ride Along Dear Grandma* (2003), *A Hand in the Future* (2008) with foreword by Belinda McKeon, and *From The Wild Wild West* (2010) with foreword by Tom Donegan, Programme Officer for Children's Books Ireland. She has read her work extensively at venues and festivals throughout Ireland, including The Maria Edgeworth Literary Festival, Boyle Arts Festival, Force 12 Writers' Weekend, Athlone Literary Festival, Goldsmith International Literary Festival, Portumna Literary Festival, Strokestown Poetry Festival, Poetry Ireland *Introductions* Series; Out-to-Lunch (Irish Writers' Centre), Siarscéal Festival, Tigh Filí Arts Centre, Mullingar Arts Centre, Ó Bhéal, Liffey FM, North West Words, Glenstal Abbey, Backstage Theatre, and Longford Library. Her poems have been shortlisted for various competitions including, amongst others, The Boyle Arts Festival, Coothill Arts Festival, Cúirt New Writing Award (2015), The Fish Poetry Award (2017), The Rush Poetry Award (2017), and received the Longford Festival Award for Poetry in 2013. She is included in the Hodges Figgis 250th anthology *Reading the Future* (2018) and in A Poem On The Dart (Poetry Ireland 2018). She facilitates creative writing for the Department of English at Maynooth University with students from the Masters in Drama Therapy, Writers-in-Schools Scheme, the Niland Gallery, The Dock Arts Centre, and the Arts Offices of County Longford, Roscommon, Leitrim and Westmeath.

www.salmonpoetry.com

"Like the sea-run Steelhead salmon that thrashes upstream to its spawning ground, then instead of dying, returns to the sea – Salmon Poetry Press brings precious cargo to both Ireland and America in the poetry it publishes, then carries that select work to its readership against incalculable odds."

TESS GALLAGHER